THE FUTURE ANCIENTS
by
Luka Lesson

Copyright

Title: The Future Ancients
Author: Luka Lesson
© 2013, L. Haralampou aka Luka Lesson
lukalesson@gmail.com

This 2nd Edition published in July, 2022

Cover Illustration by Sarah McCloskey

ALL RIGHTS RESERVED. This book contains material protected under International and Federal Copyright Laws and Treaties.

Any unauthorized reprint or use of this material is prohibited. No part of this book may be reproduced or transmitted in any form or by any means, electronic or mechanical, including photocopying, recording, or by any information storage and retrieval system without express written permission from the author.

"The destiny of man is in his own soul" - Herodotous

TABLE OF CONTENTS

Preface 7
Labyrinth 10
Amber Lights 15
Astrono-me 20
Please Resist Me 24
A to Z 28
Kaleidoscopes 35
She Wades Knee-deep 41
Scars 45
The New Crusades 48
Leaders 52
Diaspora 54
Luck (Τύχη) 56
What Have We Become Pε ῾Ελληνες? 59
Yiayia 63
Athena 67
Centre Place 71
Killing Time 75
History Books 81
Coins of Language 83
>

Elemental Spectrum   *86*
If This War is Won   *90*
The Fifth Season   *93*
The Confluence   *97*
Eloquent Abyss   *100*
Power Lines   *103*
May Your Pen Grace The Page   *106*
Feathers   *109*
Exit   *113*
The Future Ancients   *115*
The Poet's Quote   *120*

Dedicated to Caleb Jones and Omar Abu-Dabat.
If it wasn't for your departing, I may not have stayed so long.

Rest in Poetry

PREFACE

Recently, I had the pleasure of reading Herodotus' *The Histories* for the first time. Immediately I was not only imagining the vivid scenes within it, but also sensing how it must have felt to travel throughout the known world gathering stories and experiences and then finally, etching them all onto papyrus for one of the first ever attempts at creating a record, in prose, for future generations to discover. Written around 420 BC, his book is a record of oral histories, stories told, myths enjoyed, proverbs gathered and rumours solidified. It was this book that originally gave me the inspiration for the one you are now holding.

The Future Ancients is intended to be a more modern record of speech, proof of hip-hop's poetic nature, and the transcription of a storyteller's repertoire; nothing more and nothing less. It is a collection of 30 spoken word and rap verses written between 2008 and 2013. Along the way, with help from Bronwyn Lovell and Petr Malapanis, as much effort as possible has been put into enhancing the layout and readability of the content, without losing its rhythm or *spoken* feel.

Today, unlike in ancient times, individuals can each own a copy of this book, but not necessarily have the luxury of having someone recite or perform it for them. So to bring together the opportunities presented by new technologies and the growing love of spoken word poetry world-wide, *The Future Ancients* has a special feature. I have included a single 'QR' code at the end of poems to link by way of an easy smart phone scan to videos or audio recordings. Since spoken word is an oral tradition, YouTube has become something of a library, connecting us directly to poets and their performances. This QR code is meant to facilitate this connection more easily.

Above all, this book is for the teenage me. For the kids who never really got 'poetry', but thought hip-hop was amazing and were never told they were essentially the same thing. It is also for everyone who has ever helped me in ways, big or small, since I began writing. Thank you all so much for supporting this work, and more importantly, thank you for being a part of my journey.

Much love, Luka

LABYRINTH

featuring Hailey Cramer

Born in an earthquake
I learnt fate was nothing but a cross between my search and
my birthplace
Blood from Meltemi winds that speak to me
where the mountains meet the sea
on an Island of dreams
I mean

East of where Minoans first made mosaics
West of where Jesus once spoke Aramaic
North of where Hypatia taught algebraic
South of where Athenian theories were formulated

I
couldn't believe my eyes when I found the Labyrinth
in the ground
wet from clear water running down the mountain
I'd never seen a labyrinth
how was I to establish
it was grounded in a battle
like it was a map of Nazareth town?

The Labyrinth grew from earth
from patterns in the dirt
heard a battalion converge
I heard the call of birds

We're all born into a labyrinth at birth
we're all born into a labyrinth at birth
on a search

Come follow me
I will guide you in to the middle
every step you take
every mistake you make
I will guide you in to the middle

Escaping execution
I ride to retribution
two moons in the sky
a diamond in my eye
an eagle by my side
a letter from a beggar telling me to turn six lefts
and twenty-seven rights

Assembling the evidence
on a quest to find the centre
of this elaborate
labyrinth

I've been banished to the desert
where I resurrected a Bedouin
he's telling me the essence of why I'm eloquent
and how we're heaven sent

And then he let me know:
"Be as powerful as the owl that glows
and as wise so that you never choke"

Before he left
he gave me many letters and notes
and taught me how to read the sand dunes
like a Rosetta Stone

And that was hieroglyphics
so he reminded me that writers were invited
to fight at the Olympics
with their lyrics

He said: "The earth is made up of words;
it's a labyrinth of knowledge
we all enter at birth
on a search"

//

I walked forthright
I paused
caught sight
of four knighted horsemen drawing swords in the torchlight

All four corners of the labyrinth were in plain sight
so I remained calm
took the reins
and got my aim right

I shot straight past
they made way and chased hard
I prayed to the grace of God to lay the path

Cobble-stones
had gotten so
grotty, no-
body knows
where the Autumn snow shows
or where our footprints go

They started shooting guns
I knew that they had won
a bullet through my lung
just like a setting sun
and like a setting sun
my demise is my rising
when seen from the other side
of the horizon

So as I hit the dirt
reminded me of church
I took Communion from the crust of the earth

We exit a labyrinth at death
and it's the same one we enter
at birth
on a search

Chorus written by Hailey Cramer

AMBER LIGHTS

The boys at school and I disappeared between classes
passed tobacco between our hands like water at the well
smoke signals provided translation
between multi-coloured kids
                wagging in a vacant lot

We met there between family and school
                      felt most at home in the no-man's land
where the old and the new worlds couldn't find us
We even met there for fights
first kisses
        swigs of alcohol on weekend nights
It's even where my friend Mark told me about how our friend
Omar
had died
and I found the truth somewhere between the explanations

Us kids grew up in that vacant lot
between being Greek
Lebanese
Vietnamese
and Australian

Knowing we were no longer truly either one
but somehow both
Migrant kids are like rivers
always moving
but somehow still enough to be given a name
like Wog, Nip, Fake - hyphen - Australian
So of course when we learnt how to drive
we'd ride for hours in the only place where we felt like we
belonged
somewhere between points A   and B
between the green and the red
I learned to love the traffic lights when they turned amber
because I realised our teachers also slowed down on their
approach to us
and tapped their feet impatiently for our answers

I've learnt to rest my head in the elbows of my lovers
somewhere between their hearts and their hands
like the moon
I keep my distance
because it's the only thing that makes me look like
I'm standing still enough   to get close to

So now I write my best work in transit
in hotel rooms where the linen is transparent
and the paintings by no-one

I write so the silences between my words can begin to make
sense and I exist somewhere between the surface of the
page
and the tip of the pen
so I wrote this piece   in the margins
but the whole thing
is the TITLE
at dawn and at dusk
somewhere between the ridges
the pinnacle   and the cusp
so when they tell me I'm not political enough
             not Greek enough
       not Australian enough
not a poet enough
             not street enough
                    or not me   enough
       I tell them I am a star
and I exist somewhere between you seeing me shine
and realising
                    I'm already dead to you

I just let you witness some of my burning

I am not a hyphen
       I am a 100-metre dash
between my history
and your make believe
b   etween White-Australia policies
and being saved by the colony

                between having to drag my past, kicking, back into my
                present
and then hide it behind my back
                                in your presence
So be careful when you place that hyphen in my name
or I'll use it to cut your throat
just to show you how much I love this country
but that I will always have some *Sparta* in me

I may be the amber light
but amber is the only gemstone that is a living,
flowing, liquid - permanently fossilised
that keeps itself warm
that is used as medicine
that smells sweet when it gets burnt
that in Roman times was worth more than a slave
that was used to decorate Mycenaean tombs
that was named 'ήλεκτρο' by the Greeks
a precursor to the English word for 'electricity'
because they discovered that if rubbed the wrong way
amber will always create a spark
and amber is only ever *increased* in value
when some of us
are discovered   stuck   in   it

So of course us forgotten ones
                                        the in-

betweens
         the most rare

would gather around the fires in that vacant lot
share fleeting moments of belonging
and tell stories   in our silences
of how our friend Omar was sent flying
between the hood of a Holden
and the wall of a house
        like a shooting star

I'm just glad we got to witness some of his burning…

ἤλεκτρο— 'electro' the ancient Greek word for amber

ASTRONO-ME

From the 'Big Poppa'
the Big Bang
me and Hip-hop
became friends

Silhouettes in the sweats of our dance
revolutions in the pops and the locks of our hands

Zero gravity
a spin cycle
competitions for nothing but street titles

We're all stars
all spark like lighters
some burn for longer
but some burn brighter

Life,
with my eyes rose-tint
I even tried to spark my own flint

They tried to kill me in the blink of an eye
but in time you'll catch a glimpse
of my glimmering and glint

I'm a diamond in a sky
I let it shine on the page as a sign of the times

I don't follow the stars so don't bother me
I light my own path

Astrono-me

The universe in my verses
each word like the earth
'cause it's curved and it's cursive
each letter is a star
how many constellations in a paragraph?

Each wish that is cast in the distance
is crafting a gift in our hearts
but our master
is asking each of us
to commit to looking after
the star on which we've been cast
in the darkness

Our dice have been thrown
it's the rock we call home
we don't know what we've got
'til it's gone
like the trees in the Amazon
or the bees in the honeycomb
when every season is sunny though
we'll know the end is on the cards
and even our debts
will be worth nothing but a joke
like a funny bone

They want to colonise Mars

//

So will I make all the money and the perks?
and will it take me to the edge of the earth?
I only want to be a star so I can change all the hurt
but how many sins do we make on the way to the church?

You better face it,
it's certain
to engage with a certain kind of person
you've got to meet them halfway
balance on the line like a circus
between your anger and your purpose

Make a parody to make them purchase
make them love you first
before you make them nervous

They say I've got the world on my shoulders
like a burden
but I'd rather be hurting
and making a disturbance

than falling for diversions

so while I'm making the conversion

between a rolling stone and a star
I know I'll keep burning

even when they close the curtains

PLEASE RESIST ME

Please resist me
colonise me
compromise me
and conflict me

Please don't risk me
if you see me at the airport
please
come and frisk me

Please resist me
colonise me
compromise me and conflict me

Please don't risk me
please call me stupid
because your resistance
brings my evolution

Please resist me
call me a wog
it's brought us so close together
I could call me a squad

Please resist me
lock me in solitary confinement
I'll close my eyes and admire the quality of the silence
I'll write rhymes in my mind honestly and define them
solidly redefine and memorise them
until like a diamond
when I come out
I'll be better than when I arrived in

Please resist me
keep me under the thumb
keep me downtrodden
keep me under the gun
keep me working harder under thunder and sun
son - haven't you heard?
I'm becoming a gun

Please resist me
because resistance
brings evolution
and you've resisted me so consistently
I thank you for your contribution
I am a happy man
your stupidity has made me strong
I've developed wings
a thick skin
and this here opposable thumb

It holds my pen which loads my explodable tongue
so without loading a gun I'm killing high quotas of
unemotional...
punks

Sorry
you also taught me to speak French
I learnt it when you kept keeping me at arm's length
and then I learnt Italian
just to expand my head
and Greek to learn from where my ancestors had fled

And then I learnt some Yanyuwa
just to show the people of this land some respect
you see
it's been your example that has led me
to leave you
for dead

So don't trust me
I'm risky
insurmountable unaccountable
I'm an undeniable unreliable maniacal liability
I fire soliloquies and my liturgies literally leave a literary
litany

You see
when I was little
they told me I was

illegitimate, illiterate and limited
little did they know that in a minute I'd be killing it
I'm vivid like in cinemas
so my synonym is vividness
I stick it like I'm cinnamon and kill it like a militant
I live it like a citizen
you live a life like imprisonment
besides Indigenous, immigrant might be the most legitimate
of citizens
so it's better to live a life like us

Isn't it?

Language of the Yanyuwa nation from the South-West Gulf of Carpentaria, Australia. Taught by Yanyuwa elders in Borroloola and at the University of Queensland, Brisbane.

A TO Z

Apple
aardvarks and alligators
an adlib ace
an Adidas appreciator
an astrophysicist as apt as Astroboy
my apostrophes and asterisks act as asteroids
as Athenian as an acropolis
as armed as an Afghani
an Aboriginal apologetic
as anti-American as an Al-Qaeda army

But for Barack Obama he did once brandish a beautiful brain
besides we both broadcast our breath to blow-up
Bush's Bagdad base
bureaucratic Big Bird brains
bi-lingual Bin Laden belittling bureaucratic big birdbrains

Courageously creative on crates
committed contemplator
Captain Cook critic
cross-cultural communicator
a connoisseur of Chuck T's
common sense and Cassius Clay
committed to colonial change like Castro and Che

Distinctly dashing
donating durational dictations to the disadvantaged like
dreams
don't do drugs, drink or damage
develop dictionary destinies and determination
democratic dialogue
dictatorship disintegration
definitely don't dumb it down
deliberately delivering didactic detonations

Emotional elephant
evolved from earth's elements
effortlessly eloquent
exceptionally excellent
eminent embellishment
enemies effeminate
emcee etiquette expert
with an elegant exoskeleton

My **F**amily's forefathers foresaw
their fortunes would fall
they fought for flights for four
for them I find my feet firm on the floor

God
green grass
glue
Greek greetings – Γιάσου
graffiti
great gargantuan goo
gun-gripped gripes
gifts from girl guides
government guidelines
geishas, gestation - grew
groper gills go great on George Foreman's grill
gypsy guitars grieving ghosts of Guadalupe from Germans at Guernica

Heroic haiku hustler
humble hypothesiser
Hellenic heritage holder
hip-hop highlighter
headphone hijacker
a hermit, a heretic
heart healer
headache holder
Hippocratic hypocrite

Impeccable impetus
impatient and immune to immoral internet
illicit and yet innocent
intentionally intimate
I ignite ideas inside intentionally ignorants

intent upon imprisonment
I'm impatient in imparting ideologies Indigenous and immigrant
and I insist on injecting ink instead of insulin

The **J**ibber-jabber justification of justice
I'm just as dutifully juxtaposing the jury and judges
I'm joyfully jovial on my journeys and jaunts
with my jacket, jumper, jersey, jewellery and jihad jaw
my jugular's a jungle of jinxes
a jurisdiction of jokes to give
Jack and Jill the jitters
like jelly fishes
I jump at joints by J Dilla, Jay-Z and Jurassic 5
and my job as a jukebox is just to jot jests that jeopardise

Kapow!
kendo, karate, kung fu
Kuwaitis, Kazakhstanis, Kenyans, Khmer Rouge
koalas, kangaroos, kookaburras in Kakadu
The KKK killed King and Kennedy - they're cuckoo.
Kaboom!
kaleidoscopic kamikazes in Kabul
Ned Kelly's kinsman keep keeping their Kingswoods
Kremlin KGB keep Kurds on their knees in Kosovo
komodos in kimonos kick karaoke in Kyoto
kids in kaftans keep kebabs in their kitchens
Kentucky Fried kids keep Krispy-Kremes in the kingdom
ketchup and Kit-Kats

kilograms of kilojoules
K-Swiss Kanye kids use a 'k' when they spell 'kool'
Kazantzakis and Khalil Gibran; keys to knowledge I keep
But I am an artist
much more Frida Kahlo than Keats so

Learn a language
let your lobe and larynx
learn to let your lungs and lips
levitate lyrics

Motivate to master mantras
move to memorise metaphysical messages

Nocturnally nurture notations
nurse notebooks in narrative negotiations

On
one occasion
the omnipotent One opted to offer His own oration
one oracle's observations:

The **p**eople's prophet was poised to preach to the public
from the pulpit
I paused to paraphrase the paragraphs of the poet

It's **Q**uiet
the queen questioned
and quintessentially He quickly quips a quotation
I quote it:

"**R**ap requires a revolutionary renaissance
a rhetoric reincarnation - a revelation!

Something simple so when Simon says:
'stay strong'
society simply sings the same song"

To the theatre
the teacher talks tremendously to teach the thespians
that trials and tribulations of T-Pain
are treacherous
treason-tongued track tapers are testing

Us
unequivocally unfaithful underdogs are underestimating us
understating us
using utterances
undercutting unity
us

Versus vehemently vain ventriloquists
virtually viral vehicles verbally vetoing victory
vocalists
vitalise vocab

With wise words weathered and wrinkly
we want wisdom within the West
warriors with weapons well weighted and widespread!

We want an

X-ray of xenophobic

Youth
yammering Yankee yabber
Y-generation please just yabber you
with

Zeal
zap zany zealots
and zealously zigzag
alphabets
from Zakynthos to Zaire to the zoo in Zagreb

A
to
Zed

Γιάσου – Hello, Goodbye

KALEIDOSCOPES

I remember
my parents once read me a story
        and bought me a kaleidoscope.

The story was about a boy
and the kaleidoscope was one that you could see straight
through and use whatever you were looking at
      to make the patterns

I would take it outside and stare at the sun
        or point it at a cut on my knee
   like I was performing surgery

I used to love looking at my parent's faces
when they would get me into trouble
      they'd turn into confused
                  supernovas
inverted universes
of angry eyebrows,
      my mum's jewellery
          and my dad's moustache -
     cut up
       into fragments

From then on life came at me from all angles

bones were broken
>	grandparents disappeared
>>	I was asked to become a giant

and I was taught that my imagination was a fool playing with
nothing but broken windows,
>	like they were pieces of ancient puz zles

>>	Jagged edges
>	reflections of light
>>	shards of stained glass,
>>	It's the little things in life that matter.

So now I throw pebbles onto pages and play hopscotch with
memories hoping the right ones will stick

Have you ever done that?
decided on which memories to keep
>>>	so that in the future
>>	you'll be more happy with your past?
I remember being told that each drop of water we sip
has passed through every single human that has ever lived

that has ever taken breath

our bodies are mostly droplets of ancient history
currents of calamity,
>	tsunamis of circumstance,
>>	springs of inspiration.

The Pharaohs of Egypt used to say:

ىنات عجري مزال ليننلا هايم نم برشي نم

"whoever drinks from the Nile, will always return"

So as I grow may this river inside me, clean me
like ashes to the wind

smoke billowing through my canopy
                                      sand along my brim

                Shards of stained glass

My mother remembers me as a one year old, singing to myself…
humming in my play-pen with my fingertips covered in my own used nappy
I was painting the wall with my first ever masterpiece

                      she says I must be an artist at heart

So when my love finally came to me
                    in our bed a forest grew

and grew until our ceiling hung with vines
                      and the walls became the world all around

And our hearts

         sailed back over a year
     in and out of weeks and through a day
                  until finally we felt like we could look each other
right in the eyes and say

     Be.   Still.
                    ...and it would work

with not so many jagged edges
                         but reflections of our own hearts
She smelled like the crushing of crystals
          on the rocks of self-love

Clear, but thickening the wind.
          "l'amore e com'e' la luna" she said
          "quando non cresce, cala"

          "Love is like the moon
          it is only ever either growing stronger
                    or fading."

So she set off into the forest
          where fifty bedtime-story-high buildings
     cast shadows   all over her naked body

she set off into the forest
               where the f i l a m e n t in her heart
glowed brighter with each
step   from   our   edge

        she set off   into the forest
where one man's outback,
        is another woman's in front.
Where one woman's wilderness,
           is another man's home.

So she never really spoke to me
she just heard me in her dreams
and ta l k ed to me in light
while I licked her filament clean

I was hoping to be a natural man
a tree trunk   or a wave
a spider   in her web
encased in the geometry
      of her frame
           but instead...

Have you ever done that?

Decided on which memories to keep so that in the future
I remember
my parents once read me a story and bought me a
kaleidoscope

So now I listen to the words of the fool and gather the lost
pieces to my puz zle
I make sure the shards of glass are valued for every hue
        bad memories for their self-
    reflection

        cuts like bars of light
and I have learned to build a kaleidoscope in my mind

learned that I am a Rubik's cube
                      a mosaic
               a geometric pattern
                                  a
                               labyrinth
     I have learnt that I am a
               cathedral
not a broken window
we are all tsunamis of circumstance
               currents of calamity
                        springs of inspiration

No matter how many jagged edges
or shards of stained   hearts

I remember... I was asked to become a giant

but where the wild things are...
we come in all shapes

and sizes

SHE WADES KNEE-DEEP

written in Aotearoa for Deborah Jones

Your mother turned her back on your father's hospital bed
and prayed for his safe arrival
"The cancer had done enough
to be able to push it over the line" he said
and he decided that today
        was going to be the day

So he clenched his toes and fists
closed his eyes and tried his hardest to end it
like he was giving birth
        to his own death

Your father had to be patient in the end
and let life drain from him   like a king tide

He said he was excited to see you
and that you'd been more successful with this before

Who knows which metaphor would be the best for him?
Koha
Nazareth
Green stone
Tiki
Rotorua

And your simile -
Silver fern
Jesus of
Koru
Eternity
Manaia
    Now, your mother wades knee deep
at the beach
where both yours and your father's ashes are scattered
where they mingle with the bubbles
where they carve themselves into my nostrils
with the scent of every cliff calling me
               to dive with you

You
Gang Member
Peace Maker
Mountain
Monster
Comedian
Carcass
Dealer

dealt

And in your reflection
she wades knee deep
she talks to you in all kinds of silences
hears your wisdom in the crashing of every second wave
        and your father speaks in every other

but she sees you
giving out Communion on Sundays
as she makes her confessions in the back row
waiting for you to pick her up by her tears
stretch the single wing she has left on her heart
and let it flap in circles
                              not falling
but laying dormant on the stack of love letters you wrote to
us
    each one   a blade

things falls backwards up mountains when mothers lose their
children
every tree grows into the earth with its roots to climb
        her cups of tea boil frozen

so she wades knee deep

She's just happy the water level has fallen somewhere below
her lungs
                          I tell her I'll get a tattoo for
you

but there and then I decide not to have a tombstone
peppered on my skin in remembrance, so as to make it easier
to forget.

So I walk into the water
with her,   I wade knee deep

I wash my face and hair with you,
bend down
                        and swallow your reflection

Twice

Koha - gift, offering

Tiki - a figure in Maori/Polynesian culture usually made of carved greenstone

Rotorua - town in the North Island of New Zealand/Aotearoa

Koru - a spiral shape based on the shape of a new unfurling silver fern frond symbolizing new life, strength, growth and peace

Manaia - a figure usually depicted as having the head of a bird and the body of a man. Traditionally believed to be the messenger between the earthly mortals and the domain of the spirits; its symbol is used to guard against evil

SCARS

for Cristine Cuttaia

In the city
scars fall upon us without warning
through debilitating accidents
acrimonious attacks
and love

And to feel better in the morning
we are reborn through self-hate
and an impossible escape
to another love

Left screaming at the gods for inventing pain
we continue sharpening our blades
and blaming ourselves
and that love

But I believe we are blessed with the inner reflexes for
initiation
to gain scars

I believe our humanity asks us to be torn
and shattered and graced with razors

The brain is a muscle and muscles must be damaged to grow
strong
'That which does not kill me'
we've known that old adage for so long
so scar
but rip your wound so open so wide
you walk as if inside out
so your heart sits on top of your ribcage proud
and is no longer just worn on one of your sleeves every now
and then kid me with your kidneys
become known as a liver
wear your guts like a scarf
so you're never known to shiver
deliver your soul
so you don't need to speak it
you just draw diagrams with your diaphragm and lungs
so your stance handsomely lands upon the tips
of their tongues

Scar
get your guilt amputated
precious pretences surgically removed
jealousies scalped
so your intestine's true intentions shine
and protrude

Prove your intelligence with your skeleton
a bone through the nose
so they know that what you know lives in your bones and it shows

use your own skin to make a drum to beat
your hair the strings on mandolins to make it strum and sing
of your
Scar until you're covered in scratches
until the scratches get so dense you're covered in patterns
then scratch at the patterns until there's no space in between
until you're so covered in scars that it looks like you're clean

Then scar your pages with your stationery
but don't you dare stay stationary
move
leave track marks on every page you choose to lay your

scars

THE NEW CRUSADES

Do you know how war goes?
Feeding on the lost souls
Do you speak in Morse code?
Or do you speak for man?
Have you seen the new day?
Killing's on the news page
and we're all in this crusade
while we live on black man's land

They say that it's hocus-pocus
but I know that they're overdosing
on posters opposed to hope
and supposed to denote the pope
as a post-colonial local

They're loaded with quotes from the Bible
King Solomon's own survival
I jot it in pen, my saliva's
more salty than all of the eyes
of the children of mothers who've died
in attacks
from Afghanistan troops
with their battle camp boots
and a pack of canned soup
in the back of their troop carrier
packed to the roof
with a vat of C-2
their jacket
their crew
there's a new king
but it is their coup

New government
the judge and jury love it
they put the truth in the cupboard
so the public won't discover it
you
think you'll uncover
but you never really touch it
and it's proof
that we're all puppets
in this Punch and Judy covenant

Love
can't get enough of it
more loving for the sufferers
the lovemaking's a break
from all the cussing
and the hustling
right?
all the tussling and busting at night
crime and punishment
well it's rhyme
and nourishment time

Do or die
are you reading between the lines?
It is no man's land
if you stand between me
and a mic
a meaningful life
so let this genius write
it's like I'm Jesus
Houdini and a genie
combined
when I'm reading the signs

So while you whine
I turn water to ink
I'm all talk for the cause
that's how I force them to think
they want me to go to war

like Immortal Technique
but I'm not immortal, man
I'm just a mere mortal
who speaks

They say it's the pen
versus the sword
but that is so boring
because our pens
are just our compasses
and may we always be exploring

So while we picket signs for our rights
and try to Occupy the streets
we all must be very careful
how we justify
a fight
for peace

LEADERS

*from 'Leaders RMX' with L-Fresh the Lion
and Farid Farid*

I'm just trying to provide some leadership
inspired to be aligned with leaders
engaged in a dialogue with their demons

And shining through the right allegiances
no pretence
they don't pretend to be geniuses
just walk the talk in their speeches it's
Médecins Sans Frontières - Doctors fighting diseases
Emmanual Jal travelling the whole world
fighting for peace
it's just
some of our leaders can't even leave the streets
they need to compete to be feeding their seeds
they've got no time for dreams
they fight day and night for something to eat

And to dodge the police
and watch all the lucky ones leave
and not let it stop their belief
there are no greater leaders than these

Times haven't changed
dangerous minds lay isolated

stars align and constellations lead to the same old
conversations
                      Land

The constant craving of man to take by force
demands the sands of time be laden with land mines
and replaced by ports
resources
are way too important
the labour's imported
fake leaders drag us to war
by calling the poor
the terrorist forces

Real leaders leave a space for us to walk forward beside them
real leaders won't drag you down just so their status can be
heightened
real leaders don't police your speech when they decide it's
wrong
real leaders lead us all to freedom
and keep us strong
long after they're gone

DIASPORA

Απ'την Ελλάδα ο παππούς μου τραγούδησε
<<Είμαι πρόσφυγας ξερίζωμενος ρε>>
Πήρανε δρόμο με τη μανά μου μικρή
Από Διακοπτό, Μονόλιθο και Παραδείσι

<<Καλό ταξίδι και καλή τύχη>> από
Πελοπόννησο και Ρόδο νησί
δύναμη στην ψυχή,
και τσιγγάνες καρδιές
όπου πάμε καίμε λιβάνι

Fate went
this way then that
it swayed like the boat they saved so long to catch
lives packed
cases stacked
looking back
black in that they knew they'd have to re-enact the Iliad

Ill, sad and already homesick
denying the fact they were leaving their homes
just to be homeless
a small stash
that they'd never get home with
in love they interact
but they know that it's hopeless

They see the harbour and it's as cold as ever
so they both
hold my mother by her hands together
so they can
find the strength to say their boldest έλα!
and drop down on the streets with a soul to set up a
new city
a new life - διασπορά

Keep tight pride is needed inside our hearts
these acts would teach me of the past
και τους λένε <<καλή τύχη όπου και αν πας>>

From Greece my grandfather sang
"I am a refugee who has been uprooted"
they took to the streets with my mother still a child
from Diakopto, Monolithos and Paradisi

"Bon voyage and good luck" from
the Peloponnese and Rhodes Island
strength of spirit
and gypsy hearts
wherever we go we burn frankincense

έλα - come on!

διασπορά - diaspora

και τους λένε <<καλή τύχη όπου και αν πας>> - and they tell them "good luck wherever you may go"

LUCK (Τύχη)

They told him he would make it
παππού don't see the end
they told him "take a ticket"
say a goodbye to friends
he kissed his mama sweetness
before he left for Egypt
his mama's my papa's papa's papa's mama
it's deep shit

So deep I hardly speak it
a little fear in pockets
a little silver locket
a lot of tears up in them sockets
those diamonds from the eye
aligning stars upon the night
and frightened by the lonely light
that's shining through the smoked horizon
Alexandria, was only just the first stop
from Egypt came a month at sea
sent like mail to a post box
like a letter with no envelope

just enveloped by the rain
the tears of ink drain
replace the canvas on the frame

They landed on the island
no welcome note or hug
the sky as grey as Melbourne
the earth as red as blood
Μετανάστες on the ocean
bags packed for the night
a night turned into life
I return to make it right

I throw my luck upon the ground
so she can feel the earth
give her thorns to wear - it hurts
so we remember birth
wrap her body up in flames
just to drop her in the sea
my luck and me, we argue over memories

They walked from village morning
for days to get to boat
they left from olive trees
in a puff of shisha smoke

That place from which they came
dangerous because of snakes
until they brought the deer and they became the symbol of

the state
Italians colonised
and the Turks, they'd been there too
crusaders built cities on cities of the ancient few

So when my people left
never to return
they'd sing them songs of magnets
that pull them on a search

And so the greatest of the great
lucky country, cutting trees
man to man
like he was slicing nationalities
in a country of animals he'd never seen
a snake found him and pulled my παππού to his knees

I throw my luck upon the ground
so she can feel the earth
give her thorns to wear - it hurts
so we remember birth
wrap her body up in flames
just to drop her in the sea
my luck and me, we argue over memories

παππού - grandfather, or in this case, great-grandfather's brother

Μετανάστες -migrants

WHAT HAVE WE BECOME
Ρε Ἑλληνες?

What have we become since we said <<Ὀχι!>>
Ρε Ἑλληνες!?
and what is it we have said "Yes" to?
If our Jesus met a Muslim man, ϱε Ἑλληνες!
would he say: "You are God's son and I bless you"?

Who are we to think we are better?
did we not suffer Turkish rule?
did we not learn that to hold a woman underwater
is to also suffocate the heart of the cruel?

Or did we say <<Ὀχι!>> ϱε Ἑλληνες!
to much more within ourselves?
did our φιλοξενία turn to xenophobia
when we took arms and gave them hell?

Do we not know how it feels to be victimised?
did we not suffer at the other's hands?
so why do we want to victimise
and 'do unto others' as they did unto us again?

Did we not survive well in the caves, ρε Έλληνες!?
outlasting the hardest of times?
did we not sing and dance and pray, ρε Έλληνες!
no matter what the pain was in our lives?

Did we not collect the olives and grapes and drink their juice
and brine?
Did our wine not taste as sweet as the kingdoms we worked
to undermine?

Were our lives not as full as theirs, παππού?
was our culture not as real?
when they had us by the throats, παππού
tell me we could still feel

Tell me that we still had that something
and in the future we still will
tell me our culture is not only based on whether we are
occupied
or on who it was we killed

Tell me my people are strong enough
not to be trapped by our thoughts and minds
still fearful and angry at an internal enemy
we should have left so far behind

Tell me my identity doesn't depend
on whether or not I hate a Turk
and that our God is wise and strong enough
to welcome him in my church

What have we become, ρε Έλληνες!?
has the wisdom of our elders
turned to an arrogance of being better than the rest
when you cut off the rest of the world, ρε Έλληνες!
you cut your head off from your chest

Slaves manned our democracies
wars have littered our lives
I can no longer pray at the Acropolis
because the church says she no longer sings my ties

But our εκκλησία is in so much pain, ρε Έλληνες!
my priest struggles to connect
to break through his contingent's prejudices
and show 'the other' some respect

But I dance and I sing and I pray, ρε Έλληνες!
I drink my juice and brine
I burn λιβάνι on my altar
I allow my tongue to speak of life
no longer does a 'Turk' or story of a painful past
have the power to hurt my life

I am sorry γιαγιά and παππού μου
but to be a victim one must victimise
I'm not prepared to continue the cries
nor does it do us justice to act exactly like those we despise

We are our only enemies now
the only one that ever exists
but if we keep pointing at the other
our inner enemies we will always miss

This is what war does ρε Έλληνες!
Από τον πόλεμο
this is what we have become
the victims always lose
and the winners
always think they've won

Ρε Έλληνες - You Greeks

Όχι - No

φιλοξενία - hospitality

παππού - grandfather

γιαγιά - grandmother

εκκλησία - church

λιβάνι - frankincense

Από τον πόλεμο - from the war

[Refers to 'Οχι day' - a national holiday in Greece celebrating when Greek Prime Minister Ioannis Metaxas said "No" to an ultimatum given by Italian dictator Mussolini during World War II.]

YIAYIA

My Grandmother
grew up between two wars in Greece
lost her brother Christo to the Germans
and named my mother Christina after him

Rare for a Greek woman, she had a divorce at fifty
and has lived for thirty years by herself
with his photos still in the spare room
she is a green thumb

she makes cordial from her own mandarins
drinks tea from her own chamomile bush
and picks tomatoes from her garden whenever I say I feel like a
σαλάτα
she hardly went to school
but one day when talking of my time at University
and admiring all three different types of basil she has
growing in her garden

She says to me:
"Luka, eat two leaves basil every day
good for the blood
good for the brain
they don't teach that University"

And when my brother Eliah says to her:
"You know *Yiayia* - you know a lot; you're really smart."

She always replies:
"Yes Eliah, I'm a very education!"

So recently I decided to ask my *Yiayia* what she thought
about racism
and whether it was OK for some Greeks to still hate the Turks
for what they did to us in the past
and she said:

"Just because some people naughty, doesn't mean you throw
the rest in the rubbish"

Her name is Katerina Batounas
but her maiden name is *Sarandavga*
Sarandavga literally means 'forty eggs'
and as the story goes
one of her great-grandfathers
was challenged by another villager
to see if he could eat an omelette made with forty eggs
without getting sick

Anyone that knows my appetite
will know that I'm proud to say he won that bet
and so his nickname 'forty eggs'
then turned into the family name
and was passed down the generations
to my *Yiayia*

and today
it's her birthday
so I tell her what we always do
<<Να εκατοστήσεις>>
'May you live to one hundred'
but she is 83
so instead of thanking me she says
"Oh God me!
A hundred?!
No thank you, I have enough
maybe couple more years - then I go to sleep"

Where will you go to sleep *Yiayia* ?

"In the cemetery - I already I buy a 'lilli' house there.

I don't afraid!"

Until then
she will keep calling me to see if I am too cold when I'm
visiting Melbourne
keep stopping me from doing the dishes
after she cooks us a meal
keep trying to slip me a fifty dollar note
every time I visit
and keep telling me:

"Eat two leaves basil everyday
good for the blood
good for the brain "

They don't teach you that at University

σαλάτα - salad

ATHENA

Αθηνά
the goddess my ancestors once worshipped
still sits perched upon the columns of the Acropolis
make no mistake

The circling bird that would sit on Socrates' shoulder
whisper into the ear of Pythagoras
and who wiped the tears from my
great, great, great, great, great, great, great, great
grandmother's face
came to me
right after my Trojan War
as I laid upon the ocean floor
covered by the weight of my own tears

By a crevice of brothers
who I've lost who should now be men
a shipwreck of another I may never trust again
and that barnacle-encrusted rubble of a love
that should have never come to an end
she came to me

She loomed as large as my own pain
spread her wings to be the size of my own faith

and motioned me to take from her
that which would now be used to inscribe my own name

She closed her eyes as I grasped the feather
and hardly quivered as I ripped the quill from her chest
"Take it"
she said
and as I did
I saw the millions of ships that she'd witnessed
thick with my fellow countrymen
soldiers and pirates
all writing notes home to their wives on lines of papyrus
I saw
Homer writing *The Iliad* and Οδύσσεια
Προφήτης Ηλίας writing love letters to Medea
Αχιλλέας reading scrolls to the minions
and Plato just taking a note
before he voiced an opinion
I saw them all
And at that moment
Apollo stood forth
took the quill from my hand
took the black sticky ink from the most ancient squid and
filled it
and said:
"May this ink come to your defence
as it has for this old squid against every fisherman
who has ever lived,
as it has for every anarchist

freedom fighter and activist
they'll tell you 'actions speak louder than words'
until your words make people
act
like
this"

And at that moment
King Κωνσταντίνος stood forth
and sang:

«Χριστὸς Ἀνέστη εκ νεκρών,
θανάτω θάνατον πατήσας,
και τοις εν τοις μνήμασι,
ζωὴν χαρισάμενος»

<<*Λουκάς Χαραλάμπος*>> he said

"Your name means 'light, joy, illuminated'
your first name is the same name as the first saint
who painted the first icons that line our churches
and are worshipped every day

You shall not be afraid!"

And at that moment
the ocean began to fall
the waves crashing above me began to look like clouds again
and I began to feel something like
proud again

All of my ancestors stood forth and said to me:
"Luka, write with this quill
so that when your great, great, great, great, great, great,
great granddaughter
is in pain and needs to be freed
may you then come and stand with us
so we all can give her
exactly what she needs
May our air
in your lungs
speak new words
with your tongue
<<Σήκω πάνω>>
stand up son!
You have only
just
begun"

Αθηνά - Athena
Οδύσσεια - *The Odyssey*
Προφήτης Ηλίας - Elijah the Prophet
Αχιλλέας - Achilles

Christ is risen from the dead,
by death He conquered death,
and to those in the graves
He granted life!

Λουκάς Χαραλάμπος - Luka Haralampou

Σήκω πάνω - Stand up

CENTRE PLACE

Melbourne Poetry Map: Audio Graffiti Commission

Αμάν! Αμάν!
Outside the alchemist
at the crossways of the tides
across the cavernous divide of the coastline
lies a passageway of passion where we all collide

Your own boredom is about to commit suicide
as you traverse through the universe's own small intestine
through the belly of the beast
the marketplace, the cardamom, the cinnamon, in the
colours of Matisse...
Centre Place
the citadels sliver of hope
in the depths of the centre of her earth
where foreign tongues who spoke frankincense and myrrh
now speak in frankness as they lay submerged

Cross into this mudslide of cultural divides
of course the southern corner
of the Majorca building has been Jack London colonised

but that is where the takeover ends
and we transcend into fusion

The Greek makes the best crepes at *Aix* - No illusion
The ground loves to ache from being staked with high heels
 - Absolution
The healthy eat fat steaks and pieces of cake - No gluten
The congregation break bread and talk of sex
- No Communion
Italians quote Confucius
Parisian lights enlighten our delusion
Everyone's sexy set against the pollution
and the cigarette smoke and the light combine to make the
whole place look translucent

Watch the beautiful women and men float past in a
thundercloud
as the claps of lightning in our eyes lay shrouded by the other
sounds
Just how underground we are gets hard to tell
but you can take the gate to the right and climb upstairs into
Hell

We're down the bottom
the deepest point of the path
where the holy trinity is a coffee, a cigarette and a spark

This is where a homeless man only asked me for a pen and
some power to change

and drew a watch on his wrist and wrote the word
'Now'
on its face

And I did the same

It's where the whole world congregates
on the left, in the last corner
where Origin call-centre workers
watch the pilgrims cross over the border

so cross
But as you step through those gates into the arcade
walk downstairs even deeper into the caves
into the centre of our existence
where all languages are made

It is the beginning
when you speak
it's like your own Big Bang

Once we speak we are born
so after feasting on the perfumes of this kaleidoscopic
sandstorm
go and choose a script from the crypt
And pick your next life's new form

Μπράβο σου
έκανες μια βόλτα
και που θα πας τώρα;
πάρε μια γλώσσα
ο χάρος σε περιμένει
πήγαινε και να σε καλά

είσαστε άνθρωποι του κόσμου
είμαστε άνθρωποι του κόσμου

Αμάν! Αμάν!
We are the people of the world

Αμάν! - Mercy!

Bravo
you've taken a stroll
where will you go now?
take a language
the ferryman is waiting
go and be well
you are people of the world
we are people of the world

KILLING TIME

featuring Candice Monique

Can't you see?
time isn't of the essence
you can't measure love or lessons
with hours, minutes, days or seconds... no!
Life cannot be told by time
what's infinite will never die
and life goes on while we're not keeping time
so it's time for time to die

Minute that I feel this beat
minute that I feel the need
minute that I need to hustle
minute that I need to speak
minute that we let this start
minute that I feel my heart
minute that you're feeling me
is the minute that we get to spark

Minute that you're feeling Lesson
minute that I'm feeling blessed
minute that we get connected
is the minute that we get respect

Sixty minutes / tick
they consistently kill us / tick

the minutes diminish
they pillage the villager's will and their pillars of hope / tick
I never got into that rope / tick
I never got into that boat / tick
I mentally ever got better and never let enemies get in my
road / tick

A lie

The truth is I just died a million times
but in my mind I let the devil stay disguised in God's design

Tick
tick
tick
emotional moments
alone with my only opponent
just the ghost of me
I'm close to imploding
supposed to be focussed
so I spray my own cologne for atonement
and hope it exposes
the road that I've chosen - Moses

Because the truth is I'll survive
when my gods and my devils shake hands and toast to life
when my angels and my demons love each other
through my eyes
and we never bow down to the father they call
'Time'

//

Hours that I spent alone
wishing for my time to go
hours I spent on the road
hoping on a sign for home
hours I spent trapped in thought
Who I could be
Who I was
What's my mission?
What's my cause?
power taken
hours lost

Hours I spent on my mission
wishing on my time to glisten
hours I spent in conscription
fighting on the right inscriptions

Sixty minutes / tick
But time is infinite / tick
the ticks don't even mean shit

it's kind of ridiculous
the way that we fit to this
dissidents
bliss in the release from this prison
they say we're killing time
but time is killing us
and she'll never be leaving no witnesses

We grow old
but the older the better
the colder the weather the better we learn to weather the
storm and hold it together

Never being handcuffed by a clock on my wrist
and I will never be addicted to watching the watches and
clicks

They say time is of the essence
but that essence is us
sunrise
sunset
that's all we need - that's enough
we time our whole lives to a paradigm we don't trust
we don't realise that that paradigm was designed by us

And the word 'clock'
comes from the French word for bell
but when will the bell toll for time?
I guess only time can tell

//

Now that I've changed my life
now that I've made it right
now I can play the dice
now
just in case I die
now, not the past or future
now I see past illusion
now I don't cast assumptions
now I only see solutions
now I am a present man
the only gift I understand
is the present of the present
only 'now' is the time at hand

No more minutes tick
no more hours called a day
no more years
taking months
taking weeks
taking my faith

Let's go back to the basics
the earth revolves with the moon
the sun joins the two
gravity makes it smooth
oceans rise and fall
babies learn to crawl

winter, spring, summer, fall
seasons change - so do we all
and the poets record it all
people die and are kings
messiahs to fiends
in the silence I dream
that if Christ knew His life would mean
we'd count every second
and His death marked the start
He'd discount it in a second

Every culture in the world
had its sense of time
the West erected Big Ben
like its sense was mine
it's time for the rest to connect
and question why
the truth's in the moment
the rest
is memories
and lies

Chorus co-written by Candice Monique

HISTORY BOOKS

I'm sick of hearing about Captain Cook
he was not the worst of the bunch
check in your history books
he had orders to show Indigenous people respect
it's just a pity that he landed with a cargo full of convicts

Who didn't care about respect
they were fighting to survive
they came from a city where rats could eat you alive
and they were full of pain themselves
they'd just spent months in a cell
trapped with chains and gangrenous health
and brains full of hate

And that hate spread like a wildfire
and it they took it out on every black man, woman and child
their brains were full of Darwin's theories of evolution
it formed the basis of executions
and that's the basis for this artistic revolution
because no man is better than any other man or more advanced
look what we've done to this place
and tell me we're more advanced

No we are not
we were wrong
that's the sound of change my friends

For the first hundred years we had a frontier landscape
with no laws to follow or cops to enforce a mandate
and by the time there were laws and things became illegal
the government gave the public guns to kill Aboriginal people
because they were 'squatting' on pristine white farmland
and now we've all got rich
we can sit and judge them from our armchairs

The same thing happened with the Nazis didn't it?
where my ancestors were marched up a mountain and
pushed off a cliff
that's what happened to the ancestors of these Aboriginal
kids
so now we make music just to share a common reason to live
and if an N.T. teacher doesn't care about what their history
is
you think they're gonna go to class and listen to shit?

You better listen to this
because hip-hop and poetry are the only places
a real education
can still exist

N.T. - Northern Territory, Australia

COINS OF LANGUAGE

National Gallery of Victoria
and Melbourne Overload Poetry Festival Commission

As coins fly over their heads like bats in summer
rivers swell to bursting as though the ground cries

Cicadas warn the people of the dangers
because nothing is more terrifying than to have your
language scraped from your lungs
and to be forced to use your oppressors' words
to articulate to them the depth of what they have done

"Always was, always will be Aboriginal land"
could be translated into all of this nation's Indigenous languages
so it stays rooted in the earth
before histories haunt us like ghosts
but have no way to tell us who they are
before whole libraries commit suicide
and come back to tap us on the shoulder
but cannot tell us their names

Language, a finite resource is being extracted from
children like zinc
letters like shards of lead
words like gold
sentences of silver
paragraphs of iron ore
Dreaming story uranium
proverb purple opal
each lung a shaft
each rib a beam
more blood pumps new reserves
each vein a seam
each tongue a pick
each eureka a dream
each shovel a pencil
each stalactite a pen
each voice-pipe a tunnel
each truck a letter sent
each shipment a vocabulary
each elder a mountain
each son a new reserve
tears like diamonds
every lament a crack
every war-cry an explosion
each death another shaft collapsed

and while they sleep, coins fly over their heads like bats in
summer
precious stones are sold and resold

and dug up and resold and dug up
and resold
And more cuts are opened up
and more cuts are resold and dug deeper
and resold and dug deeper
and cut up and opened up and dug deeper
And shifted and sorted and melted down
and shipped to the port
and shifted and sorted and melted down
and shipped to the port
and shifted and sorted and melted down
and shipped to the port
And moored and measured and made clean
moored and measured and made clean
and moored and measured and made clean to be
placed in white frames and encased in a glass
placed in white frames and encased in glass
placed in white frames and encased in glass or on white walls
for the upper class

Open cut mines pillaging raw lungs
the money pours through white pores
Black tongues lick at the land like a salted lake
just to get a taste
of their own dirt

And as they sleep
the coins fly over their heads like bats in summer

ELEMENTAL SPECTRUM

*National Gallery of Victoria
and Melbourne Overload Poetry Festival Commission*

The original people
hold the kaleidoscopic heart of this land
both mirror and window
coloured by geography
permeated by pigment
laced with luminescence
carved with veins of river red
bronzed as hawk
silver of river gum
gold of wattle, ochre, sun
mauve lips like flowers
bathed in orange sunset

one young male
grey kangaroo
with tail

darts across the countryside
he sees
        purple
orange
 red
yellow
        purple
 green
                silver
green
mauve
        purple
 red
  orange
                red
 black
green
                green
 green
   yellow
        purple
he bullets over the crimson earth
and under the
blue white white
blue white white
blue white
blue white white
blue white white
yellow white blue

He stops at the slither of a snake
Young Grey is frozen by the incandescent canvas of the impressionist
as the snake's chameleon skin flickers
it switches between
black necklace on red scales
black necklace on red scales
Black stripe
sepia
black stripe
sepia
black stripe
sepia
Mustard yellow and midnight fleck
mustard yellow and midnight fleck!
Ivory speared fangs feed poisonous pearls of wisdom into the young grey
ripped from the wound shiraz droplets splatter
onto white ochre

mixing into pink;
a blushing memory of the moving image,
now still-life.

And the people
called into existence by the Seven Sisters
crafted by the sentient
sculpted in sentiment
scented in metallic as they talk both star and sand

black in blood
grown army green since white flags arrived
but never surrendered
standing under the same
Blue white white
blue white white
blue white
blue white white
blue white white
yellow white blue

Skin of salt
breath of fine yellow
holding kaleidoscopic hearts
geometric diamonds
flawlessly both transparent and reflecting
both mirror and window
permeated by pigment
laced with luminescence
elemental spectrum
Archaeological dig
for rainbow

IF THIS WAR IS WON

You don't know
you don't see my pain
'cause we don't speak
we don't breathe the same
and you know it
when it's over 'cause
they don't give a cent about our
love

I have seen
I have dreamed for change
and we have hurt
we all have scars and chains
but I don't know if when this war is won
if I'll see the moon or be the sun

He hit the street so hard
he passes the guards
past the hard labour
past all the bars

he's past it at last
the Pastor tells him "Pass your regards"
his heart's full of scars
his father left a bastard like Nas
larceny starts
and he's casting his craft
harbouring carts
the last man to be standing
shafting his staff
hardly in harm
while the rest are in danger
he checks out the mirror
sees a stranger
cursed for life

He hits the street so hard
passes the bar
past the bartender
past all the staff
he starts in the bath
finishes up the last of a flask
he's half plastered
cigars have got him raspy like Nas
faster than Nos on the arse of a car
he blows up quick
like he's a part of Hamas

The guards grasp and a glass blasts into shards and it scars
a last gasp and the guards cast his arse on the tar

"Who'll get the last laugh bastards?" he asks
In halfa' the blast from his car
scar the glass and facade
the gutter is marred
by the blood and the smarts of the guards
by the start of March
the guards' fathers are plastering plaques

Hearts at half-mast as the hard-arsed bastard is cuffed
behind bars his apartment is dark
he's asking the guards for pardons and heart
but he's hardly in harm
he checks out the mirror
sees a stranger
cursed for life

THE FIFTH SEASON

I wrestle with my demons
in the attempt to take control
at midnight
the fifth season
when even the summer's burning cold

I've been staring into mirrors
trying to mine my eyes for gold
I guess that's why I drink these spirits
because I'm searching for my soul

I've lived upon this dirt
dodging cracks in a tangled search
frankincense has burnt beneath my skin
I've wished upon the birds

I've heard voices in the moon
seen their faces in the waves
so when the tides are at their highest
they spray their verses to my page

I've had those oceans rise and fall for me
the doves fly in with the bats
I've had no-one come to lend a hand
and hundreds stand to clap

So I've convinced myself of my own genius
and I've hated with a passion
every second word I've written
so my pages read in patterns

I've learnt the thin line
between speaking and staying silent
there's no difference between keeping quiet
and just preaching to the choirs

I am the hopeless and the hope
the spoken and the choked
I'm the place to pray to make it mend
and the way that it first broke

I am the message to the rest of us
to never look inside
unless you're ready to know your position
in the consciousness of life

So I am exactly where I want to be
and I've almost killed myself for the chance
so I hold the responsibility
that comes with finding answers

Γράφω ποιήματα στον ήλιο
λόγια πρακτικά
γράμματα για τους Έλληνες
που δεν μιλάν' τα ψέματα

Έχουν καρδιές
που δεν φοβούνται τα πουλιά
θα σκοτώσουμε τους κλέφτες
και φωνάξουμε τα κρυφά

I have spoken to the earth
in so many different tongues
I'm sure she only knows me
from the volume of my lungs

She has spoken in the clouds
I hear similes in the leaves
metaphors in the now
desires in the breeze

I have listened through my skin
osmosis through my tears
I have focused with my body
her smoke has burnt me crystal clear

because this search is not a stepping stone
a journey or a path
this search is a letting go
back into the shapes we were first cast

Because we all wrestle with our demons
in the attempt to take control
at midnight
the fifth season
when even the summer's burning cold

We all stare into mirrors
trying to mine our eyes for gold
I guess that's why, sometimes, we drink these spirits
because we're all searching
for our souls

I write poems to the sun
practical words
letters for the Greeks
who don't speak lies

Who have hearts
that aren't scared of birds
we will kill the thieves
and shout secrets

THE CONFLUENCE

We met
at the confluence
where my air
in your lungs
spoke my words
with your tongue

Where my hair
curled down your face
touched my lips
but carried your taste
where your dress sat on my hips
and my lipstick was your lips
where your jeans
wrapped around my legs
and I was on my knees
when you needed to beg

Where my hair grew from your pores
Like it was your beard on my jaw
where your makeup softened my complexion
and your most honest moments
felt like my confessions

Where your figure
was my body
where you made some mistakes
so I said 'Sorry'

The confluence
where the words 'I' and 'You'
became useless
so 'I love you'
just didn't do it
we just said the word: 'Love'
and then sat in the silence to prove it
Where my knee under your skin
joined my thighs to your shins
and my ankles joined your legs to my feet
and we walked the same path where we promised we'd meet
Where your heart
under my rib cage
beat your blood through my veins
and my veins fed your arms with my reactions
until we couldn't tell the difference between us
in passion

The confluence
where my lids covered your eyes
and your teeth clenched in my mouth
where my sights were all you saw
so my fears became your doubts

Where your left hand joined my right
when we came to pray to keep this love alive
where your hands definitely cut my wrists
but I still called that
suicide

The confluence
where when it was over
only half a face was left
and half my skeleton lay broken
half my heart beat half a pulse in half this chest
and less than half my words were spoken
half a bird seemed to chirp half a song in half a tree
where 'Us'
became 'You' again
and 'We'
became 'Me'.

ELOQUENT ABYSS

They told me I could make it work
I wasn't ready for your heart to burst

The explosion of your lungs
the erosion of our love

They told me I could make you fantasise
and in effect resurrect the painted canvas I
had splattered with my heart
patterned with the stars
I'd fashioned it in glass

It was glowing 'till the winter came
until the sun made way for the winds of change
I still pray for the simple days
though you're to blame
I hope you're still the same

They told me love was gonna be a cinch
 "As long as you talk
you never feel a pinch"

since then every flame has made me feel a singe
next time we hang out
is if I'm being lynched

Because I'm drowning in our memories
going to ground like a penalty
you're making lovers of my enemies
I'm just trying to be a better me

I'm seeing double now I'm never sober
two of you is like a four-leaf clover
and no good luck just good lies
I roll the dice
snake eyes for my road signs

In the mist
eloquent abyss
I see you twist
illicit assist
if you kissed then I'd be your bliss
but since we missed
I guess I'm just a risk

They say commitment is a test of fate
so I search my own doubts and assassinate

Though I know you think you told me the truth
a real truth hunts down a lie
and executes

And even though you're cute
your talk didn't stand up
so I take aim and shoot
they say that's what a real man does

And when the clouds cry
we let them storm
and when the grounds dry
we know we're getting warm
I found life - I'm getting born
and when the birds fly
we let them swarm

This is not the way to make a start
this is not the way to break a heart
this is not the way to make it last
if you're coming first
I'll take the last

POWER LINES

Written for 1/6's album Electronic Mail

And through the weathering of words
my throat bubbles with the tiniest murmurings of hope

Streams of consciousness remind me of my own lunacy

In my darkest hours I still turn to the tools like farmers to
ploughs
I reach for pens and these sheathed pieces of tree that we
believe can hold the weight of our pasts
and still somehow carry us into our dreams

My digits dance at the foothills of screens
iridescent they reflect syllables back into my own pores
a clenched jaw
so the lyrics are swallowed and pushed out through my arms
so I don't need to write but these keys begin to read these
palms

As I push forth scars at low-tide
birds swarm outside
ready to pick similes from between my eyes
and feast on metaphors disguised by *Rappertags*
and battle cries

Sequels of our own lives will be played in reverse
to highlight when it was we stitched welcome mats into our
verses for these curses
that will bear our own demise

So let us speak of our own pain and triumph
let us criticise and pave defiance
let us look into the river for guidance
and build shelters for our homeless minds in silence

But let us not let each other slip between the thunder cracks
or suffocate in the weightlessness of outer space
as we try to become stars

We are artists
let us sing each other's choruses
back each other up on every verse
and teach the kids that the Temple of Hip-hop
holds just as much imperfection as any other church

Let us see each other's spark as empowerment
used to buzz at the glints in our eyes
to combine with the dictionaries we keep in our pockets
so we will always speak in sonnets

Too often we have seen each other's coffins
may they constantly give us the confidence to never get each
other's wires crossed again
these are consecrated power-lines we balance
across as we write

let us not reach for umbrellas
to shelter us from the rain
let us climb the peaks of discontent
and the mountains of monotony
and hold these umbrellas high in the night

because our words
can only get
more electric
when the lightning strikes

MAY YOUR PEN
GRACE THE PAGE

May your pen grace the page at the same pace as your brain
may your grey matter, from now on, no longer be grey
may you mean every word that you say
and may writing your lines be the way that you pray

Get up
step up
never let up
get your setup set up
get recording
get stories pouring
ignoring your calling and calling you 'boring' is boring
you need to be touring
what are you doing?
you're basically stewing

No space for daydreaming
no place for that feeling
no place for pacing the building or facing the ceiling
there's no way that is dealing
your brain it is stealing
and there will be no change to you
and there'll never be any change to that ceiling

I'm basically feeling that art isn't hard
what's hard is your heart
and it starts in the past
but the past is in the past
so love who you are

Pass a rush of blood until your arteries blast
and let the blood rush to your arm and let your artistry start

May your pen express upon the page every feeling you're in
may your white page - yang
love your black pen - yin

May the ball in your ballpoint roll
because that's the point of the ball
and if we can't make our points
then what's the point of it all?

May the lead in your lead pencil
lead you astray
we've spelt it L-E-A-D because we've made leaders this way

And I know it's hard but easy to say
but I mean what I say
when I say: "Mean what you say"

Potentially my pencil be the deftest thing you've ever seen
adept at expressing everything that you've never seen
especially when you question me

my pencil
man, she gets to me
she comes to me and comforts me and takes me out to lunch
you see
we have a cup of coffee
before I know it she's on top of me
she's rocking and she's rolling me
we're touching uncontrollably
she likes to switch the roles on me
I think I'm writing with her but she is writing with me
it's my life as I desire to be
it's only right that she's my wife 2B

She takes me to her bed of white
we try it in the dead of night
pages till we get it right
we make love between those sheets

May your pen grace the page at the same pace as your brain
may your grey matter, from now on, no longer be grey
may you mean every single word that you say
and may writing your lines be the way that you pray

FEATHERS

for my unborn son

My child
when you are born you will be golden
you will be the salt of the earth
you will be blessed with an omen

you will be

you will be glass
shimmering steel
an eagle awaiting its feathers
an idea made real

you will be healthy
you will be joy
you will be blessed
in love, you will be wealthy

you will be loved
you will be lost
you will be finding
you will be young
and you will be reminded

you will be my heart
my breath
my new start
you will be my planet
my pearl
my craft

But the truth is
you will not be mine
I will be your father, your rock
but your mother and I
are merely guides

I will provide an arrow
a blueprint
a shape
a sign

and your mother - the river
the map
the chrysalis
the bliss
she
is love
the eternal kiss

But I can't be true to me
and truthfully
try to tell you to be
a new me

It's your life; you make it
wherever you'd like to take it

Though I'll give you your clothes
and show you your soul
you'll face your demons naked

Though I'll teach you control
and keep you from cold
if you see your chance; you take it

Though of course I have fought for you
walked to all four corners
and talked the truth
I know
my path isn't right for you
I'll just try to give you the right tools to use

because this earth isn't perfect
we're all cursed with a search for purpose
we all emerge in emergencies
and hope our perfect dreams prevail perfectly

but we
can't see the sky for clouds sometimes
and can't see our lies for doubts
and I
can't see with the eyes of owls
so I can't seem to decipher this life right now

Will I be ready to raise you?
mould you?
shape you?

Will I ever be wrong to change you
or strong enough to be brave for you?

Though I'm spreading my wings
I don't know if I'm making better enemies
or the betterment of anything
and when I'm in Heaven
I'll leave you a message of eleven melodies that you better
sing
you see, your life is my everything
and my words are your medicine

so you better remember when I tell you
that I'll be shedding every feather from my wings
so you can fly further than I've ever been
you are my king

EXIT

As the sun sets
the galaxy rises like a map of eternity

I wash my eyes with the white of clouds
so I can read God's fingerprints
like dust
on her ceiling

Under the reflection of the moon
the rain is like a spiral staircase falling onto the earth
that needs to escape

As the heart of humanness hums in the canopy of city still
perfecting its call to inspiration
trees grow seeds for spring
oceans fly south for the winter

So I walk through cemeteries of hope and see my conscience
in the marble of mortality

I know the wind has a crush on me

and it won't stop until I'm caught by her currents
turned into the shadows of thunder used to resonate shards
of hearts
shot
into the atmosphere

We are all spores
blown by our ancestors
who were as unsure of us
as we are of them

So let the tricks of history besiege me as I place rubies in my
palms and set off into rough
searching for answers I know may never come

looking to capture a horizon straighter than any truth
I could possibly believe

a horizon that falls further away from me
as I take
each step
into the future

THE FUTURE ANCIENTS

In the future
the history books will study us

our cities will have been renamed
our languages slanged into something new
and this moment
will one day
be ancient

The future ancients
dig theoretical trenches between settlement and invasion
shoot rifles at each other from across the plains
and place prayers within the screaming bullets

they shroud their heads in mourning
and afterwards line their soldiers up in cemeteries like
voodoo dolls for God

The future ancients
will be encased behind glass in museums

Greek ragtag squadrons
with backpacks
gas masks
and shards of Athenian columns for weapons

will be installed in exhibitions
of either terrorists or freedom fighters
depending on who it is that wins

this time

they will stand side by side
with wax dummies of 'good men'
in shirts and ties
who never leave their suburban blocks
but are called to duty through computer screens
shooting unmanned cannons in far away places
and are called things like
husband
son
sweetheart
and Lieutenant

The future ancients
will have their artefacts locked in storage
shards of Molotov cocktails
from the Egyptian revolution
will be tagged and filed
next to Michael Jackson albums
smartphones
Playboy magazines
and the Australian Flag

The future ancients
will be found by future archaeologists

preserved and embalmed
in tequila and Chanel Number 5
alongside pop-star prophets
who thought they were somehow saying something new
this time
they will find them
praying to gods who believe in Science
on a planet of do's and don'ts
of factions and fractions of us's and them's
and we's and whatever's
and maybe never's
and never again's
the future ancients will be found in tombs
of cheap liquor

in databases of tradition

on screens called culture

as relics of broken signals

They will hardly be visited as bones
but remembered
in the symbology of pixel
and paranoia

The Future Ancients
will be remembered or lost depending on what we decide

Since democracy has been paraphrased
sustainability called primitive
refugees criminalised by the first invaders
and Indigenous cultures lined up side by suicide
in prisons
like voodoo dolls for the future
the textbooks will study us
our cities will have been renamed
our languages slanged into something new
and our stories will be the only link left
between objects
and their meanings

They will try to twist and turn our histories
based on what they find of us
so our voices are the only artefacts worth keeping
alive

So whose lips will we honour?
on whose tomb will we lay our tears?
those that risked everything to speak
but spoke anyway
those that gave meaning in the darkness
those who not only spoke
but gifted us a moment of silence in this madness to so that
we could learn to hear
ourselves

Those thoughts are your artefacts

Your jewellery
jade
and bronze
and your words are your monuments
your stone
and bone
Parthenon
and Colosseum
everything worth leaving behind

In silence is how we surrender
speech is the architecture of fate

So are we pharaohs of fallacies
or empresses of nothing?

What will they engrave below our statues?

In the ancient future

THE POET'S QUOTE

Don't bother listening to the poets
when you need us the most

That's when the poet's quote is about to rise within you
be patient
it will happen
from the inside out

I'd prefer to teach you to listen to yourself rather than listen to me
so you hear exactly the quote you need
precisely when you need it

I never wish to make you stay
when in your heart
you know you need to run

Run.

run without us
and let me know how it goes

I'll pin your answer on my wall,
for inspiration.

Scan the QR code below to watch performances and listen to recordings of selected poems and rap verses from this book.

Luka Lesson is a poet, rapper and educator of Greek heritage born in Meanjin / Brisbane. His work crosses between the history of his family homeland, the fiercely political and the vulnerably self-reflective. A former **Australian Poetry Slam Champion** (2011), Luka has featured at the mecca for slam poetry: the **Nuyorican Poet's Cafe** (NYC) multiple times, performed with the **Queensland Symphony Orchestra** and toured with respected UK rappers **Akala & Lowkey**. Luka has released two collections of poetry independently: **The Future Ancients** (2013) & **Antidote** (2015) and two poetic rap albums: **Please Resist Me** (2012) & **EXIT** (2014).

Luka's work has also been featured in publications such as: **Southern Sun: Aegean Light** (2011, ASP), **Poems From A Green And Blue Planet** (2019, Hachette UK), and **Solid Air** (2019, UQP). Luka has been a poet-in-residence at the **Scottish Poetry Library**, appeared at the **Edinburgh Literature Festival, Sydney Writers' Festival, Hong Kong** ere

www.ingramcontent.com/pod-product-compliance
Lightning Source LLC
Chambersburg PA
CBHW072012290426
44109CB00018B/2214